1 A village shop in the Isle of Wight,
c. 1905

2 *(Overleaf)* Vine Cottage, Ashley,
New Milton, *c.* 1885. Mrs Girling and
her Shaker followers used a room in
the cottage for their meetings in 1874

Victorian and Edwardian

HAMPSHIRE
& THE ISLE OF WIGHT
from old photographs

introduction and commentaries by
JOHN NORWOOD

B. T. BATSFORD LTD
LONDON & SYDNEY

First published 1973
Reprinted 1975
Text © John Norwood 1973
Printed in Great Britain by
The Anchor Press, Tiptree, Essex
for the publishers
B. T. Batsford Ltd, 4 Fitzhardinge Street, London W1H 0AH
23 Cross Street, Brookvale, N.S.W. 2100, Australia
ISBN 0 7134 0130 3

In affectionate tribute to my Mother and Father:
cherished links with those times

CONTENTS

3   Sunday School outing at Fleet,
c. 1912

ACKNOWLEDGMENTS

A volume of this kind is not compiled without a great deal of help, and the Author and Publishers wish to place on record their indebtedness to the following individuals and institutions who readily co-operated by allowing photographs to be copied or supplied prints. Many of them also provided valuable information about the subjects.

Public Library, Aldershot (31); Andover Advertiser (87, 94); Andover Borough Council (Public Library) (130, 131); Mr A. E. Baker (11, 84, 107, 126); Mr J. T. Barton (123, 155); Batsford Collection (42, 43, 44, 45, 48, 50, 98); Bedales School (73, 74); Miss S. Bellamy (109, 120); Central Library, Bournemouth (14, 15, 46); Mr E. R. Brinton (27, 55, 78, 148); British Transport Docks Board (58); Mrs D. V. Buckle (103); Mr S. Cooke (56); Dr E. Course (40, 61, 62, 154); Mr R. Cousins (139); Mrs B. Cross (121); Echo Commercial Photos (60, 63, 88, 108); Mr F. A. J. Emery-Wallis (6, 7, 24, 25, 86, 95, 97, 133); Fawley Local History Group (96); Hampshire County Library, Ringwood (5, 26); Hampshire County Museum Service (4, 19, 20, 21, 57, 59, 66, 67, 68, 77, 80, 82, 93, 100, 112, 113, 114, 115, 117, 118, 122, 127, 128, 134, 135, 140, 142, 144, 145, 146, 147, 149, 150); Hampshire Record Office (32, 151, 152); Hampshire Field Club (17, 30); The Royal Hampshire Regiment (29); The County Librarian, Isle of Wight (1, 13, 79); Mrs M. L. Jackson (2, 141); Mrs P. James (65); Mr E. King (12, 136); Mr A. T. Lloyd (119); Lord Montagu of Beaulieu (90, 116); Mr E. R. Moss (102, 104, 105, 124); Miss E. M. Newnham (41); Mr A. G. Parker (47, 49, 52, 111); Petersfield Urban District Council (110); The News, Portsmouth (143); Portsmouth City Libraries (Pescott Frost Coll.) (22); Portsmouth City Museums (33, 38, 76, 85, 91, 153); Mr W. Richardson (39); The Director, Royal Naval Museum, Portsmouth (23, 28); Mr E. Roe (3, 53, 54, 64, 83, 99, 132); Royal Aircraft Establishment, Farnborough (34, 35, 36, 37); Miss E. K. Sivyer (129); Southampton Central Library (8, 9); Civic Record Office, Southampton (E. D. Orris Slide Coll.) (89); Mr F. C. Stallard (106); Taskers Trailers Ltd (51, 75); Mr T. Viney (10, 81); Mr N. Wareham (101); Mr E. A. White (92); Winchester City Library (16, 18, 125, 138); The Warden and Fellows of Winchester College (69, 70, 71, 72, 137); (28) and (31) are reproduced by permission of Gale and Polden Ltd, Aldershot. (39, 56, 101) and (129) are deposited at Portsmouth City Records Office.

The Author also wishes to express his gratitude to the following who assisted in various ways in resolving problems which arose in the course of writing commentaries on the photographs:

Col. J. M. Clift, Museum of the Royal Hampshire Regiment, Winchester; Miss M. Cooper, Well-come Institute of the History of Medicine, London; Miss D. B. Edmonds, National Army Museum, London; Lt.-Cdr. G. H. F. Frere-Cook, R.N., Submarine Museum, Gosport; Staff of Hampshire County Libraries; Mr C. W. Hawkins, Alton; Dr R. H. Little, Ringwood; Mr A. T. Lloyd, New Milton; Mr S. L. Matthews, Seaview; Capt. A. J. Pack, R.N., Royal Naval Museum, Portsmouth; Mr E. D. G. Payne, Ryde; Dr M. W. B. Sanderson, National Maritime Museum, Greenwich; Mr C. J. Scott, Herbert Art Gallery and Museums, Coventry; Mrs P. Stephens, Winchester City Library; Mr M. E. Ware, National Motor Museum, Beaulieu. Miss M. C. Macfarlane, Director of Hampshire County Museum Service not only gave the project every encouragement but went to great pains in the dating of many photographs from costume detail; Mr J. D. Joseph undertook the copying or printing of most of the photographs, many calling for considerable technical skill; and Mrs J. O. Weeks gave valued secretarial and clerical assistance.

Note on dating

Wherever possible an attempt has been made to date the photographs. Where there is good evidence an exact date has been given. Where this has not been possible internal evidence has been used to give an approximate date; and in cases where a range of dates is possible the more conservative has been given.

INTRODUCTION

The essential character of Hampshire and the Isle of Wight has always been quietly rural; so much so that they have long been regarded as an archetype of England provincial, agricultural and conservative, a country-side for retreat and relaxation that in quietly going about its business avoided most of the pains and excitement of the booming nineteenth century. The raw materials here were the soil and the sea, and centuries of labour with the one created a deep attachment to the countryside, while from the other was made a highway for the nation's commerce, a rampart for its defence and, later, a means of recreation.

There is no shortage of works describing the topography of the two counties, and there can be few features of interest, natural or man-made that have not received their due share of attention; nor is there any lack of photographs which might be used in compiling a pictorial survey of them. But that is not the purpose of the present volume. The photographs presented here have been collected with an aim which is believed to be both different and new: to display something of the life of the area in Victorian and Edwardian times. In order to keep this end in view a rule-of-thumb has been adopted that the pictures should cast light in one way or another on what it was like to have lived at the time. Thus there is a strong emphasis upon human activity, or at least presence, and the few town-scapes that are shown have been included because they were part of the familiar surroundings of the time that have since been materially altered either by re-development or destruction.

4   Alton in March 1863. 'A magnificent triumphal arch of large and noble dimensions' erected to celebrate the marriage of the Prince of Wales and Princess Alexandra of Denmark

Victoria's reign saw many important developments in photography, but as no example suitable for inclusion here was found that could confidently be dated earlier than 1860, the collection effectively illustrates that half century before the First World War so brutally disrupted the way of life our grandparents knew. During that time there were numerous advances in techniques and materials. For example, the wet collodion plate which had been introduced in 1851 became very popular for its sensitivity and speed; but it suffered the drawback of needing to be prepared immediately before use and developed immediately afterwards, so that for anyone working away from a studio it was necessary to transport a complete darkroom outfit. When the much faster dry gelatine emulsion appeared in 1878 plates could be factory made and the photographer, unencumbered, become truly mobile. A development that enjoyed a great vogue for some 15 or 20 years from the mid-1850's, was the stereoscopic photograph taken with a binocular camera, of which 24 is an example.

Although some small cameras had been made earlier, it was the introduction of the rapid dry plate, followed by the first roll films in 1885, that led to the appearance of a whole range of convenient lightweight cameras for the amateur and stimulated the growth of photography as a popular pastime. Big cameras, however, remained in use with serious photographers since enlarging was a slow business and large prints could readily be made from large plates. The results were often splendidly sharp and detailed. The originals of 20 and 21 were contact printed from 12 in. × 10 in. plates, and 19 from a 13 in. × 8 in. plate. Advances of another kind came when the introduction of orthochromatic emulsions in the late 1870's and panchromatic emulsions in 1906 allowed the recording of colours in increasingly realistic intensity and so overcame the flat quality and lack of sky detail in earlier pictures.

Technical problems were not the only factors inhibiting the photographer. There was the question of what should be regarded as worth photographing, for the camera was wielded by our forebears primarily as a recording instrument which owed a debt to posterity as successor to the artist. Thus among the proper subjects were family portraits, groups of every kind, stonelayings, celebrations and important buildings; those generally regarded as beneath the camera's notice included the working man, the ordinary home and the majority of folk activities. Such was the general rule, for the professional photographer at least, and so it remained until about the time of the First World War; it is to the non-professional that we owe most of the unselfconscious pictures of humble people and everyday events that have survived. Such pictures are of particular interest to the social historian and are all the more precious for having to be sought out; they are curiously neglected in public collections where the emphasis is still on topographical recording. One particular phenomenon of the times ought not to go unmentioned: the rise of the picture-postcard

5   'Come and join us'. The Band of Hope at Lower Kingston near Ringwood in 1892

publisher. He succeeded the publisher of choice engraved views and much of the earlier work was pleasing; but as time went on he succumbed to the temptation of selling any view which could be photographed. The outcome was often depressingly lifeless.

Two kinds of pictures, then, will be found here: those forming part of what might be termed the official record of the times, and those which originally had no more than private significance. They complement each other, and in bringing them together it is hoped that a certain depth of focus has been achieved. Sadly, there remain several aspects of the life of the two counties for which no coverage could be found despite extensive searching; so one may look in vain for pictures of some of the sporting events, traditional fairs and ancient customs for which they are known. Sometimes, of course, a picture otherwise interesting has not been of good enough quality to reproduce.

Apart from the visual pleasure which many of the pictures give (though few could be classed as accomplished pieces of photography) they all have a mass of information to impart about near-forgotten aspects of local history. They remind us, for example, of vanished occupations, the beginnings of public transport undertakings, the precarious early days of aviation, military associations, quaintly-remote agriculture and unsophisticated pastimes. Local pride is a frequent theme, seen in the way friendly societies turned out with bands and banners for local events, in the deference shown towards the lord of the manor, and in the way a small town like Bishops Waltham could burst its heart to greet a boy prince. Public occasions were times to be made the most of, for they often meant a holiday and an entertainment, a break in hard-working and monotonous lives. We look back with a certain consciousness of loss, for our mobile society can never achieve the sense of community which came from ties of birth, upbringing and employment in one place.

Some striking differences are to be seen. Familiar landmarks enable us to find our place in the towns, but they seem eerily empty and people can wander about them quite unperturbed by traffic. The Square, Bournemouth, seen in 1865 (14) is unrecognisable in today's bustling centre, reminding us how new the town is: it sprang up with sea bathing and the villas of the wealthy. The early manifestations of the internal combustion engine appear primitive, the dusty streets are clearly still the horse's rightful place, and there is for the most part a refreshing absence of advertising displays. There is some obvious poverty. Clothes more than anything catch the eye, and there is great costume interest in some of the photographs; it would be tempting to include extensive fashion notes in the commentaries. Illustrations 140, 141, 80 and 42 serve to indicate how things altered between 1865 and 1914. Both sexes must often have felt intolerably hot and overdressed, but somehow the ladies endure with grace while the men look baggy and uncomfortable. A mass of smaller details will attract the observant: street furniture and shop fascias, banners and bicycles, tools and tea urns, amusement machines, advertisements, perambulators and whiskers. All add their comment on the nature of life in Victorian and Edwardian times. Some subjects have a point to make about social distinctions and social problems, others indicate a variety of attitudes to the camera itself.

It is gratifying to think that a few, at least, of those who are portrayed in these pictures as children are still alive and will find pleasure in reminiscing over times past. They will perhaps recall the smell of harness and the stamp of hooves, freshly-starched blouses and full-throated choirs, strains of the village band or the pungent odour of drying hops. Most of these faces have long since departed, but the camera has captured their likeness for us and preserved as their monument a brief moment of their vitality.

TOWNS

6   King James' Gate, Portsmouth
(1687) before removal for road
widening shortly after 1860. It now
forms the entrance to the United
Services Officers' Recreation Ground

7 *Left* Grand Parade, Portsmouth. On the left, a sentry outside the Guard Room, demolished 1883. In the foreground, memorial to members of the 8th (King's) Regiment killed in the Indian Mutiny; it was subsequently moved to Chelsea. Most of the buildings seen were destroyed in the Second World War

8 *Below* Bargate, Southampton from the south before the tram lines were laid in 1879

9 *Right* Below Bar, Southampton, about 1890. Nearly every building seen was destroyed in the Second World War

10 *Below right* Romsey Market Place, c. 1865. The scene is much the same today except for the pens of livestock

11 *Left* Market day at Ringwood,
c. 1890. Save for the cows and their
followers there is a remarkable
absence of females

12 *Below left* High Street, Lymington,
c. 1908

13 *Top* High Street, Newport,
c. 1865 and the Town Hall designed
by John Nash (1816)

14 *Below* The Square, Bournemouth,
c. 1865. Photographed by Robert Day
whose hut studio is to the right of the
church. This is now the busy centre
of a town which has developed almost
beyond recognition

15 *Above* The Square, Bournemouth
c. 1900

16 *Left* Westgate, Winchester,
c. 1875. The adjacent buildings were
subsequently removed and the road
moved to the left.

17 *Right* The Butter Cross,
Winchester, erected in the early
fifteenth century. Photographed some
time after the restoration of 1865

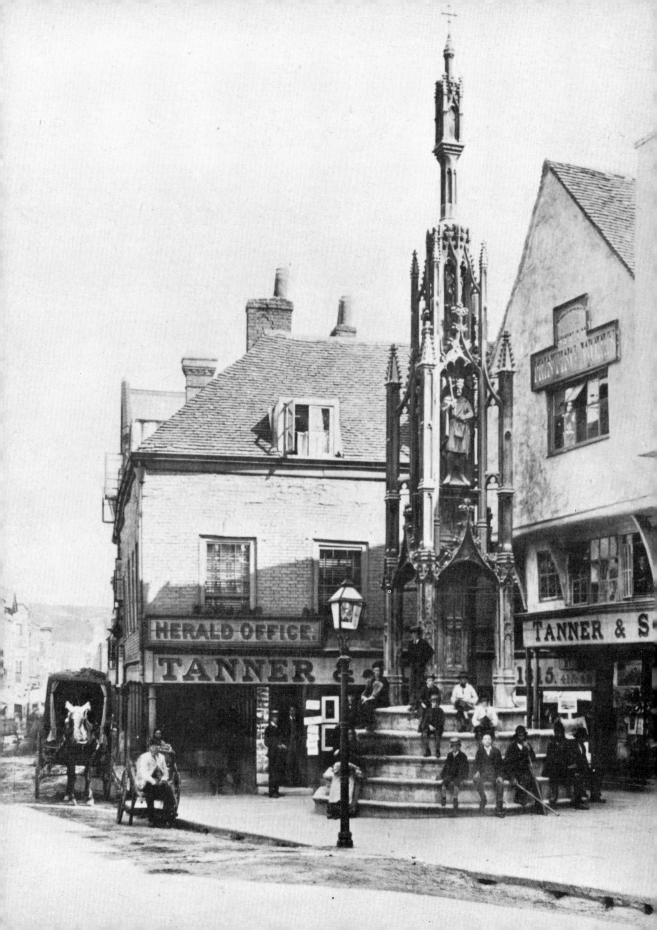

19 High Street, Lyndhurst, and the Crown Hotel as it was *c.* 1890

20 *(Overleaf)* Christmas display at an Alton butcher's, 1909. Mr Mugridge and staff await their customers with quiet confidence

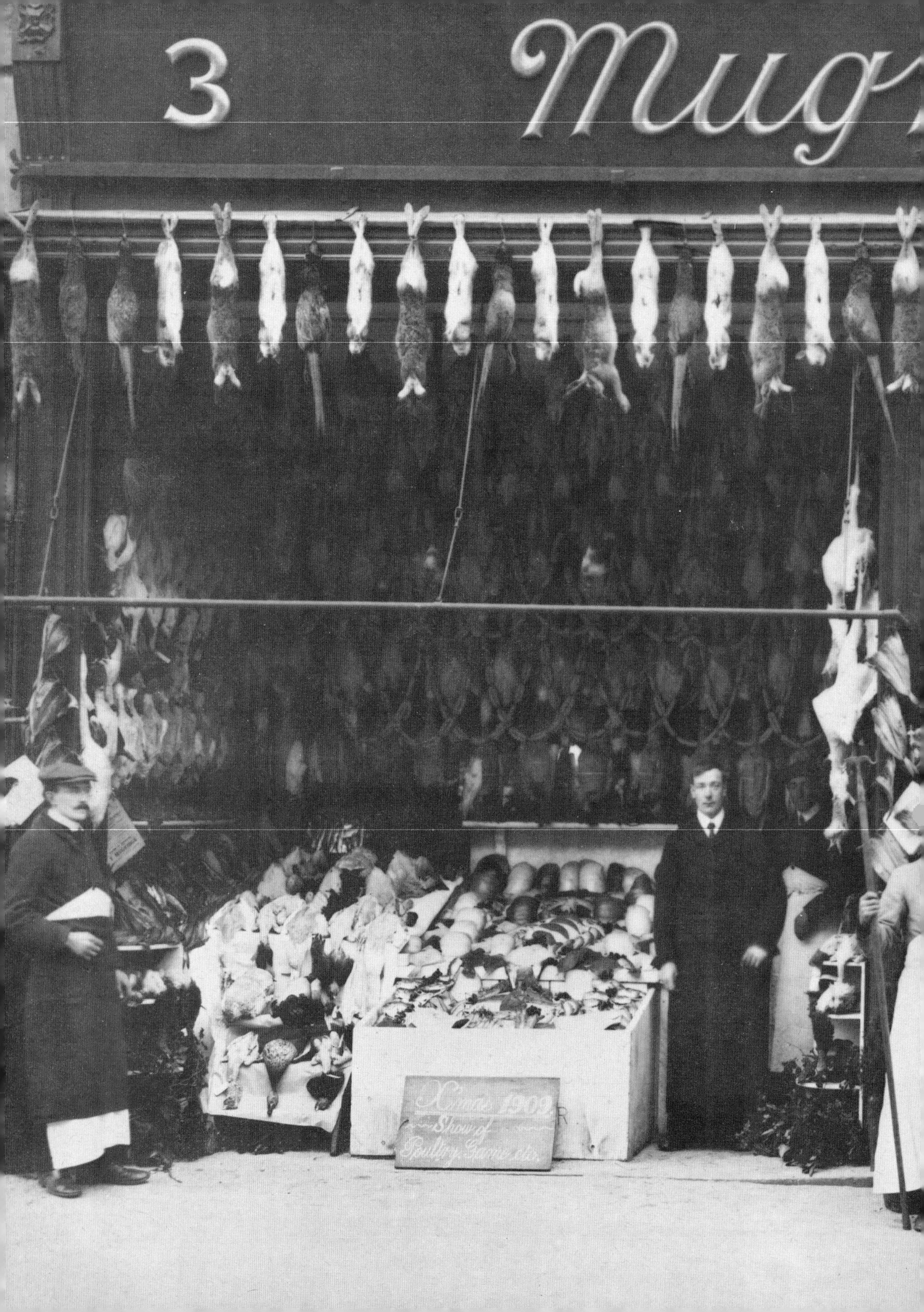
3
Mug
Xmas 1909
Show of
Poultry, Game etc.

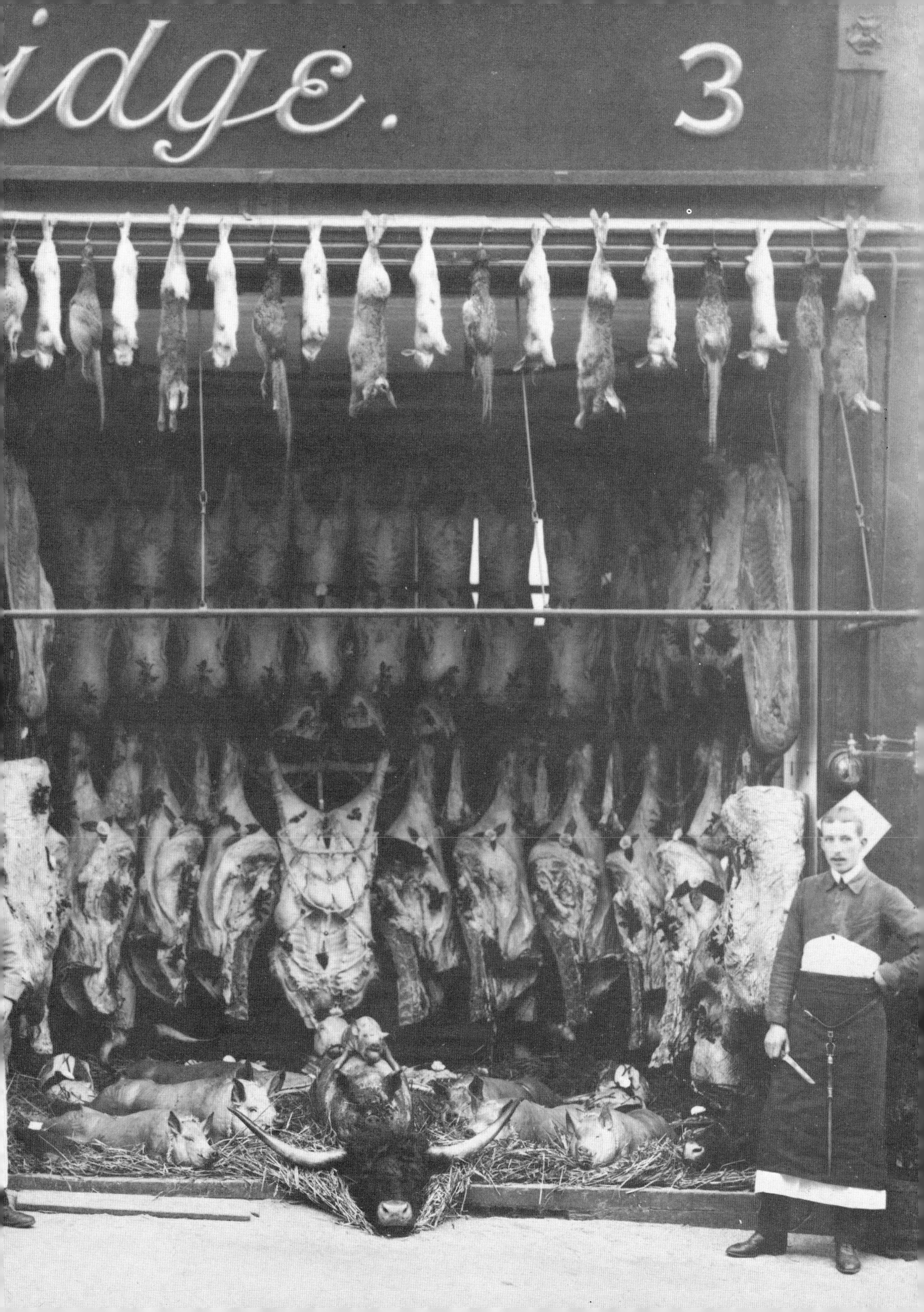
idge. 3

21 'The King and Queen Cannot
Have Better'. Butcher's shop in Alton
sometime before the First World War

ARMY AND NAVY

22 Breaking up the *Royal George* in
No. 2 Dock, Portsmouth, 1906. She
was built at Deptford for the Prince
Regent and completed in 1817. She
was later used by William IV and once
by Queen Victoria. From 1843–1901
she was an accommodation hulk for
crews of the royal yachts

24 *Left* Stereoscopic photograph of a sentry on the ramparts at Portsmouth, *c.* 1860; he is probably from one of the Hampshire regiments

25 *Below left* Men of the Hampshire Regiment trooping the colour on Governor's Green, Portsmouth, *c.* 1890

26 *Right* Men of 1st Volunteer Bn. the Hampshire Regiment parading outside the parish church at Ringwood, *c.* 1860. Notice the youthful bandsmen

27 *Below* Hampshire Carabiniers coming off the chain ferry at East Cowes on their way to mount guard at Osborn House, Queen Victoria's island retreat, *c.* 1895

28 *Below* Collecting the mail at King's Stairs, Portsmouth, in the early years of this century

29 *Right* Mess servants of the 3rd Bn. the Hampshire Regiment in the 1890's. Each holds some piece of equipment appropriate to his calling

30 *Below right* North-west wing of the Royal Victoria Hospital, Netley, built 1856–63 as the country's main military hospital and demolished 1966. Lord Palmerston wrote: 'It seems to me that at Netley all consideration of what would best tend to the comfort and recovery of the patients has been sacrificed to the vanity of the architect, whose sole object has been to make a building which should cut a dash when looked at from the Southampton river'. Florence Nightingale was horrified

31 *Right* The army's first staff car, a 1902 20 h.p. Wolseley. Seated in the rear is Major-General Sir John French, returning from the distribution of South African War medals at Aldershot

32 *Below* Bungalow residence of the first GOC Aldershot, Lieut.-General Sir William T. Knollys (1855–60), photographed about 50 years later

33 *Below* Church parade, Portsmouth, at the turn of the century. The Garrison Church is now a shell after wartime bombing

34 Samuel Franklin Cody, a Texan, was engaged by the War Office in 1904 to experiment with man-lifting kites, and became Chief Kiting Instructor at the Balloon School, Aldershot. His baskets were made a few miles away at Crondall

35 *Right* Army trials with the airship *Baby* at Farnborough, May 1909

36 *Below* Cody and an Indian friend at Farnborough. In 1908 he made the first recorded flight in Britain, and was killed in an air crash five years later

37 *Left* Geoffrey de Havilland in his second aircraft, the FE1, at Farnborough in 1911

38 C Class submarines at Portsmouth in 1909. C11 was sunk in a collision off Cromer later that year

39 Recovering grease after the launching of the *Iron Duke* at Portsmouth on 12 October 1912

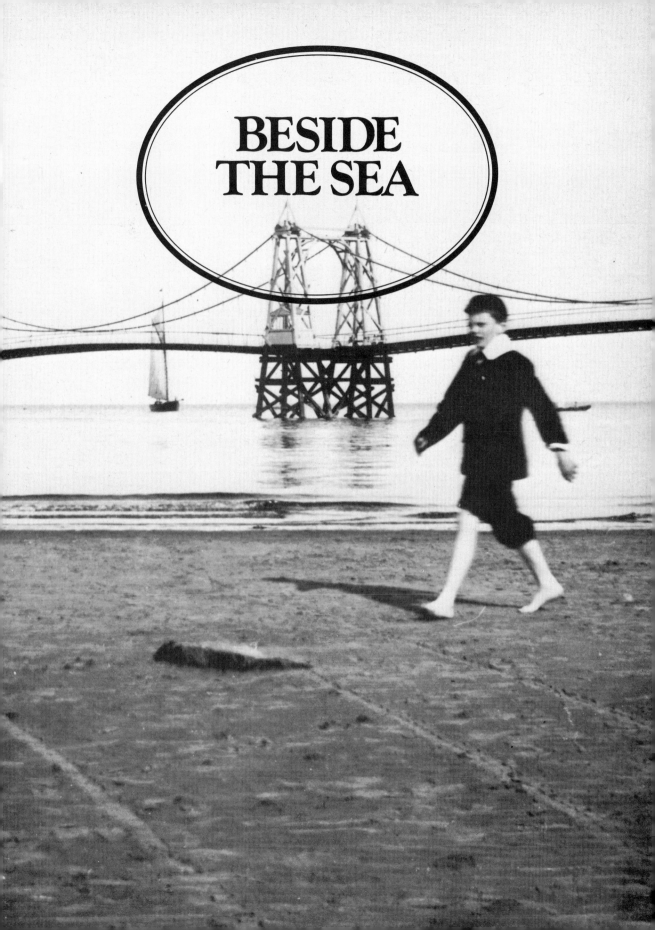

BESIDE
THE SEA

40 *(Previous page)* The suspension pier at Seaview, opened 1881 and demolished 1950

41 *Right* Sampson's Baths, Shanklin Chine, *c.* 1865. James Sampson, as well as being a bathing machine and baths proprietor, was also Clerk to the Board of Health. Notice the row of bathing dresses drying in the sun

42 *Far right* Goatcart, barefoot donkey-man and nursemaid on the promenade at Sandown, probably early in the First World War

43 *Below* The boating pool at Ventnor, *c.* 1910

44 Ryde pierhead and its dignified amusement machines. The unique paddle steamers with twin funnels abreast are the *Duchess of Connaught* and *Duchess of Edinburgh* (built 1884, scrapped 1911)

45 *Right* Cabmen's rest and cast iron frivolity at the pier entrance, Bournemouth

46 *Below right* The old wooden pier at Bournemouth (built 1861, destroyed 1878). The strollers seem to have been quite willing to co-operate with the photographer: the dogs less so

47 *Left* Paddy Hearn the coastguard at Chine Hill, Shanklin, *c.* 1890. The coastguard station was demolished in 1935

48 *Below left* Bathing machines at Ventnor, *c.* 1890. On the right, winches used to raise the machines up the beach

49 *Below* The Wheeler family of Chale, *c.* 1890 – they were noted for their lobster pots. The gap on the right and the veiled lady give this picture a sombre overtone; was someone missing? In the left foreground is a *holley* used for towing a live catch

50 *(Overleaf) Lorna Doone* at Ryde Pier, *c.* 1908. This well-loved paddle steamer, which used to sail round the Isle of Wight three times a week, was eventually scrapped after the Second World War

TRANSPORT

51 *(Previous page) Hero,* the first steam traction engine built by Henry Tasker at the Waterloo Ironworks, Anna Valley, near Andover, on its way to Southampton Show, 31 May 1869. The steersman had a warm perch; behind is a wagon with extra coal

52 The *Rocket* coach at Shanklin Station, *c.* 1879

53 Postman and donkey cart at Fleet, 1904. He is the proud wearer of six long-service stripes

54 Village bakery and delivery vehicles at Crookham in the early years of this century

55 *Right* Horse tramway on Ryde Pier in the late 1860's. It connected the pier head with St John's Road Station before the railway line was extended in 1880

56 *Below* The Portsmouth–Gosport chain ferry built by Acraman of Bristol in 1839 and in use until 1959

57 *Right* Mr Hooker, the Bentworth carrier

58 *Below right* SS *Arcadia* lying in the Outer Dock, Southampton, in September 1889. In front of her is the *Elbe*, to the left, paddle steamer *Alice*, right foreground the *Medway* and behind, the *Drummond Castle*

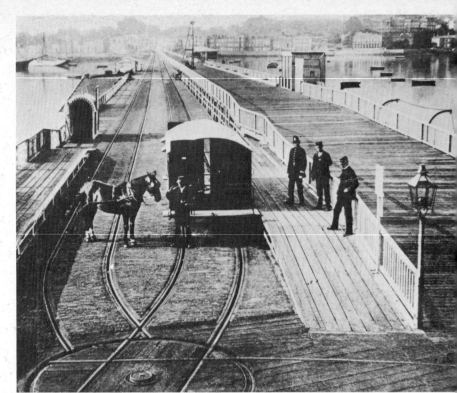

59 *Right* Bertram Stoodley of Alton with his ordinary bicycle, *c.* 1890. He was noted for riding down Normandy Hill with his feet over the handlebars

60 *Below* Royal Pier Station, Southampton, 1900. The station opened in 1891 and closed in 1914

61 *Far right* Porter and ticket collector (wearing customary buttonhole) at Northam Station, LSWR, in about 1900. The picture readily evokes the traditional dignity of working on the railway

62 *Right* Scene at the inauguration of the Shirley tram route, Southampton, 22 January 1900

63 *Below* Horse tram in Carlisle Road, Southampton, 1895

64 *Below* Liming's Garage, Crookham Village. The car is possibly a 1904 Star

65 *Overleaf* The first public service vehicle in Lymington, a 4-cylinder Thorneycroft, climbing the High Street, *c.* 1902. It connected the town with Milford on Sea at an average speed on the level of 14 m.p.h.

AT SCHOOL

66 Pupils of Meonstoke School in
1899; facing the camera was evidently
something of an ordeal

67 A winter day in the playground at the British School, Sarum Hill, Basingstoke, *c.* 1880

68 A school outing, *c.* 1889. Miss Blanche Chandler (with eloquent stance) and boys from Queen Mary School, Basingstoke

69 *Right* College football at Winchester. The game is played on a pitch of 80 × 27 yards known as a *canvas* from the lengths of canvas formerly hung along the sides. At one time there were 22 players a side, reduced to 15 in the 1880's when this scene was captured. The game is still played to rules which are intelligible only to Wykehamists

70 *Below* Winchester College Officers 1871–72

71 *Below right* Winchester College masters pose with studied casualness before embarking on an expedition to Snowdonia, *c.* 1875

72 *(Overleaf)* A group of Winchester College masters, *c.* 1865. The central figure is Dr George Moberly, Headmaster 1836–66

73 *Left* Boys and girls learning to darn at Bedales School, *c.* 1907. The school, one of the country's earliest and most notable co-educational boarding establishments, moved to Steep, near Petersfield in 1900

75 *Below* Violin class at Waterloo Ironworks School, Anna Valley, Upper Clatford, *c.* 1905

74 *Below left* A French lesson at Bedales School

PASTIMES
AND PLEASURES

76 Bank holiday fair at Portsdown,
c. 1905

77 Children with May Day garlands
and collecting box at Ovington, *c.* 1893

Please to see a fine garland,
Made early in the morning.
The first of May is garland day,
Please to see a fine garland.

(Traditional, Bursledon)

78 *(Overleaf)* Mothers' Meeting
excursion at Haylands, Ryde, *c.* 1890

79 *Right* Sightseers and a blind guide at Carisbrooke Castle, *c.* 1860

80 *Centre* Judging the terrier class at Alton Dog Show, 1905

81 *Below* Romsey Abbey handbell ringers in the 1880's

84 *(Overleaf)* Ringwood postal officials on an outing to Downton, 1908

82 Medstead brass band, *c.* 1905

83 *Below* For centuries the mummers have taken their homespun plays, a mixture of tradition and fantasy, round the inns and villages of Hampshire; here and there they have been revived in recent years. This group, in costumes of paper strips, was photographed in 1910.

Bold Roamer is my name
I have come to show you
Many sports to pass away the winter
New activity, old activity
Such activity as was never seen
And perhaps will never be seen again

85 *Right* Penny donkey rides at the Bank Holiday Fair, Portsdown

86 *Below* YMCA Cycling Club at Portchester Castle, *c.* 1890. They sport an interesting collection of machines. The tricycle on the left has remote steering with a spade grip, that on the right has a handlebar whose usefulness is demonstrated by its owner. Three high ordinary bicycles with hub lamps lie in front, and one member has brought his new safety bicycle whose foot rest suggests a fixed wheel

87 *Left* The new era in entertainment. The Electric Picture Hall, Andover; opened 1911, closed 1956, demolished 1968

88 *Below* Burnetts Lane and Durley Methodist Sunday Schools' outing to Lee-on-the-Solent 1898

89 Barnum and Bailey's Circus passing Above Bar Church, Southampton, 1899

PEOPLE AT WORK

90   Lord Montagu's gardeners at
Beaulieu, *c.* 1896

91 Portsmouth police force in 1865,
and the old Landport Police Station

92 William Moyle, shoemaker of
Christchurch, 1891

93 *Right* Alfred Trimmer (with pipe) outside his forge at Alton, *c.* 1900

94 *Below* Andover Fire Brigade with a Merryweather steam pump

95 *Top left* Loading the strawberry train at Swanwick at the turn of the century

96 *Top right* 'Granny Gritt', the pedlar, at Fawley, 1897. She collected rabbit skins and would give a yard of tape in exchange for them

97 *Below* Mr King the Titchfield water carrier, photographed sometime before the First World War

98 *Left* Jane Wort, the Overton postwoman, *c.* 1908. Despite her age she strides out with determination in her well-worn coat and man's boots. She carries her lunch in what is probably a plaited sedge basket of the kind once made in the Test valley

99 *Right* 'Old Grit', the lady chimney sweep of Fleet who was active during the First World War

100 *Below* A group of Basingstoke newsboys, *c.* 1905

101 *Left* Construction of Portsmouth Dockyard extension, 1872. Lifting power for the huge blocks of stone was provided by donkey engines on wooden travelling gantries

102 *Below* A small brickyard in Whitchurch. Hand moulders each work under a crude hurdle shelter, placing the newly-made bricks on a barrow. Behind the pump bricks are drying in hacks before burning

103 *Right* Brick makers with their moulds at Ashley, New Milton, *c.* 1905

104 *Far right* Workmen at the Whitchurch Whiting Works which closed before the end of the century

105 *Below* A country builder's yard at Whitchurch before the end of the century. The signwriter's talents are well to the fore

106 *Left* Parchment makers at Homewell, Havant. Fine parchment was produced here for many centuries: this works closed down as late as 1936. The man in the centre holds a half-moon scraper used in preparing the skins; behind, skins are hanging to dry

107 *Below* The new breed of
engineer: at work on a Panhard,
c. 1904 in Davis's Garage, Ringwood

108 *Right* Knife grinder at Bursledon.
He is virtually undateable and
represents a vanishing species. Note
the brazier and tattered bag for his
belongings

109 *(Overleaf)* Steam excavator at
work during the construction of the
Alton to Basingstoke Light Railway,
1898–99

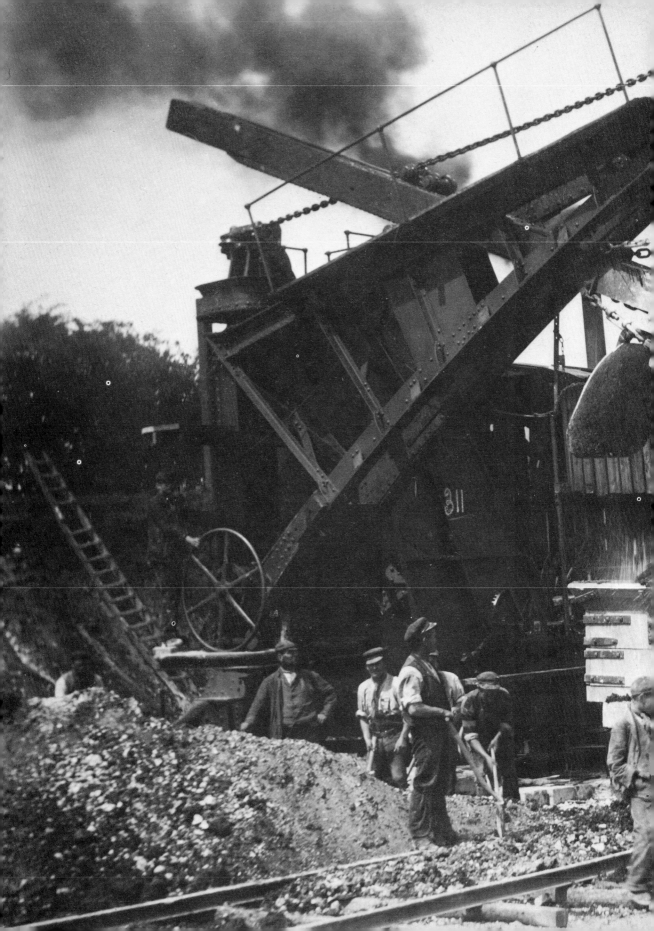

110 Women being trained to take over road surfacing, on the A3 at Sheet, early in the First World War

COUNTRY LIFE

111   Customers at the Chine Inn,
Shanklin, *c.* 1865

112 Mr and Mrs Adams of Alton, whose daughter Fanny, cruelly murdered on 24 August 1867, was the original 'Sweet Fanny Adams'

Shall I never see thee more, my dearest
*   Fanny?*
My child that I so fondly did love
Was slain and cut to pieces by a villain
But now she's in Heaven above

113 Hop pickers at Alton in 1880. At this period the vines were grown up poles which had to be uprooted for picking

114 Hop pickers near Alton, 1912. 'Hops are cultivated in long straight rows, and the whole length of one row is occupied, not by solitary adult pickers merely, but groups of pickers, whole families clustering round each bin; for the tiniest fingers can help. Baby is, of course, excused from work, but it must be there, and we find few bins by which a tiny mite is not seated in a broken-down perambulator, or in some cases hitched on to the bin itself close to mother.'
Samuel Chinn *Among the Hop Pickers*, 1887

115 Fastening a surplice of newly-picked hops at Amery Farm, Alton in 1880. The man on the right holds skewers; the foreman, left, keeps the tally

116 'Brusher' Mills (1838–1905), the New Forest snake catcher, seen outside the turf hut in which he lived. He made a living by catching snakes for zoos and research bodies

117 *Left* Waggon team on the way to Alton Station with a load of hops, 1899. Being something of an occasion, the carter has decorated his whip and the horses are decked with brasses and bells. The hop pockets are stencilled with a traditional design

118 *Below left* Reaping by hand at Tunworth, *c.* 1910. In all probability the couple here are clearing the first swathe ready for the reaping machine

119 *Below* Charles C. Dallas, celebrated New Forest sportsman, with his lifelong companion, Jack Card, in the 1890's. Dallas was still shooting in old age, supported in an invalid chair

120 *(Overleaf)* Mr Barton and shearers at Hackwood Farm, Winslade, *c.* 1900

121 *Below* Tobacco was grown at Crookham Village from 1912–37 and retailed under such names as Golden Queen and Blue Pryor. John Smith, farm manager holds a sample of the first crop

122 *Right* Ox teams ploughing at Norton Farm, Selborne in 1902

123 *Below right* Village grocer's shop at North Warnborough, 1905. The local football challenge shield takes pride of place in the left-hand window

124 *(Overleaf)* Rural poverty at Whitchurch, *c.* 1910

OCCASIONS

125 On 4 August 1864 the Queen's delicate 11-year-old son Leopold undertook his first public engagement by laying the foundation stone of the Royal Albert Infirmary, Bishops Waltham.

'We never remember to have seen so many flags, streamers, mottos, wreaths, arches, festoons &c before. . . . Several triumphal arches were erected across the principal streets, formed of evergreens and flowers, tastefully designed, surmounted with banners with appropriate inscriptions. . . . The gas illumination in the evening was brilliant and magnificent.'

127 *(Overleaf)* Saying grace before dinner in the Market Place at Basingstoke during the 1887 Jubilee celebrations

126   Arch of welcome erected on the occasion of the opening of Ringwood Town Hall, 1868, by Mr Edward Morant

128 *Right* Basingstoke Town Hall decorated for the Jubilee, 1887, when the heightened clock tower (removed 1961) was presented. It is interesting to speculate on how some of the loftier candle-lamps were lit

129 *Below* Civic solemnity: laying the foundation stone of Portsmouth Guildhall on 14 October 1886

130 *Top* Bonfire built at Andover to celebrate the 1897 Jubilee

131 *Below* The Scots Greys parading in High Street, Andover, en route to manoeuvres on Salisbury Plain, 1897

132 *(Overleaf)* A village event at Crookham Village, *c.* 1905. The band tries a few notes while waiting for the Foresters to line up

133 *Below* Gunwharf Gate, Portsmouth, decorated for the town's welcome to a French naval contingent in August 1905 on the occasion of signing the Entente Cordiale. 'The scenes in the streets, where our sailors fraternized joyously with the visitors, will never be forgotten by those who witnessed them'

134 *Right* Firing the *feu-de-joie* for the Queen's Jubilee at Basingstoke, 1897

135 *Below right* God Bless Our Queen. A rally outside the Inwood Cottage Hospital, Crown Close, Alton, in Jubilee year, 1897

136 *Right* Shop in Lymington decorated for the Coronation of Edward VII, 1901

137 *Below* King George V and Queen Mary being received at the gate of Winchester College, 25 July 1912, in the ancient ceremony *Ad portas* which is reserved for distinguished visitors

138 Winchester's tribute to Queen Victoria

139 Friendly societies parading in West Street, Havant on Hospital Sunday, *c.* 1908

THE
FACE OF THE
PEOPLE

140 *(Previous page)* The Curtis family taking tea in the garden, 1865. For much of the nineteenth and early twentieth century this Quaker family was at the centre of cultural life in the small country town of Alton. Dr William Curtis, right, founded the Alton Mechanics' Institute in 1837 and in 1855 the Museum which still bears his name

141 *Left* Members of the Browning family at Vine Cottage, Ashley, *c.* 1885. In 1874 Mrs Girling, 'Mother of the Children of God' used a room here as a meeting place for her followers of the Shaker sect

142 *Below* Domestic staff of the Curtis family in 1865. Observe the two-manpower mower which must have required a good deal of muscle

143 *Right* 'A class for poor boys every Sunday at 3'. In the 1880's Henry Blessley, a piano dealer, revived the work of John Pounds (1767–1839) the cobbler-philanthropist of Portsmouth. He is seen outside Pounds' minute shop in Highbury Street with some of his pupils whose condition bespeaks their need. (*The News*, Portsmouth)

144 *Left* Gipsy missioners in the New Forest

145 'They tend the sick, supply the most wretchedly poor with all the comforts that they have the power to give, hold services in the different camps, instruct the children, and, in fact, give themselves up heart and soul to their service'
Crespigny and Hutchinson, *The New Forest*, 1895

146 *Below* A New Forest gipsy family. The man is making a bee skep by passing straw through a cow's horn and binding it with split bramble to form a continuous coil

147 *Right* Temperance rally at Basingstoke towards the end of the century

148 *Below* Queen Victoria driving in the grounds at Osborn; the pony phaeton was made by a Newport firm

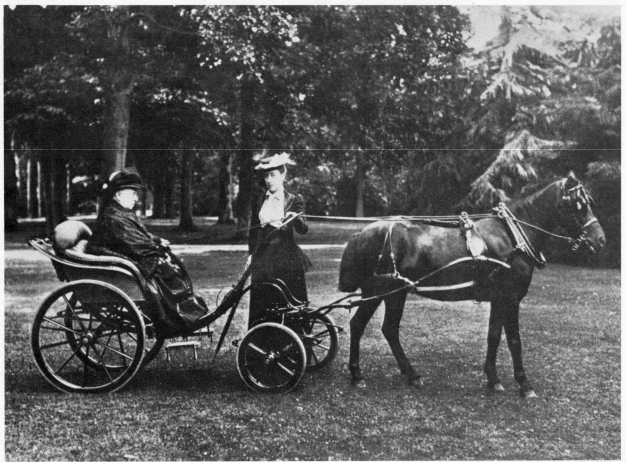

149 Sequah speaks at Basingstoke. The flamboyant salesmanship of Sequah's quack medicines was notorious in the early 1900's. A fleet of circus vans toured the country, each with its representative. After an elaborate arrival in 'western' rig, 'Professor Sequah' would produce testimonials and then go into the van to extract teeth; the band on top played to drown the cries. He would then return to sell 'Sequah's Oil' and 'Prairie Flower Mixture'

150 *(Overleaf)* Children receiving a free dinner in the Corn Exchange, Basingstoke, during a slump, February 1901

151 *Right* The Wayfarer's Dole, St Cross Hospital. The mug of ale and piece of bread, first given 800 years ago, is still available to travellers

152 *Below* Brethren of the Hospital of St Cross, Winchester, founded by Henry de Blois, *c.* 1136

154 *Top* A Southampton funeral. The peaked caps suggest that a railwayman was concerned

155 *Below* Mid-day refreshment outside the Crown Inn, Odiham. The absence of younger men suggests a possible date during the First World War